A Christmas Collection from Wales

CHRIS S. STEPHENS

Gomer

Published in 2008 by
Gomer Press, Llandysul, Ceredigion SA44 4JL
www.gomer.co.uk

ISBN 978 1 84323 979 6

A CIP record for this title is available from the British Library

Printed and bound in Wales at
Gomer Press, Llandysul, Ceredigion

Contents

The red, red robin comes bob, bob, bobbin'...

The robin, or 'ruddock' or 'redbreast' has long been a seasonal favourite. Painted, stitched and photographed against a frosty background, perched on the handle of a snow-covered garden fork, or even popping letters into a scarlet pillar box, he has repeatedly been featured on Christmas cards – the recipient of friendship, hope and even sympathy during winter weather.

His red chest is linked with fire – and not merely the warmth of winter fires. An old Welsh legend, recorded by W. Jenkyn Thomas in his classic 1907 collection *The Welsh Fairy Book*, tells of a grandmother scolding her boy for throwing stones at the robin. She reminds him that the merciful bird cools the brows and souls of those tormented in Hell, by carrying tiny drops of water in his bill to the fiery depths below. Each time he passes through the flames another feather on his breast is scorched. 'Don't forget,' she reminds her grandchild, 'one day you might be grateful for that "cool dew" from the robin's little bill!'

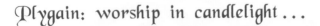
Plygain: worship in candlelight ...

Plygain, the traditional early-morning Christmas service in both church and chapel, takes its name from the Latin *pulli cantus*, the cock's crow. Staying awake for the 3.00am service was just one of the challenges; other informal competitions abounded.

Who could and make the tastiest *cyflaith* (treacle toffee) as sustenance?

Who could arrive at the church door with the best decorated, or largest, candle?

Who could compose the most original *plygain* carol in traditional metre?

The service itself, a remnant from the old Catholic midnight mass, was one of the few night-time services held, and as there was no provision for lighting, churchgoers took their own candles – specially constructed with thick wicks that would stay alight on the *plygain* procession. The candles would need to last several hours, for often as many as 30 newly created carols would be sung (some with at least 12 verses) to old English folk tunes, such as *Sweet Richard* and *Crimson Velvet*.

Lost Christmas

He is alone, it is Christmas.
Up the hill go three trees, the three kings.
There is a star also
Over the dark manger. But where is the child?

Pity him. He has come far
Like the trees, matching their patience
With his. But the mind was before
Him on the long road. The manger is empty.

R.S. Thomas

Our wassail is made of the good ale and cake
Some nutmeg and ginger, the best we could make

(Gower wassail song)

Wassailing is a well-known Christmas activity, its heart in traditions of blessing the cider trees, hoping for continued good harvests and livening up the dull days (and nights) of winter.

Besides the singing and carousing there was the important job of testing the ale, the countryman's 'wine tasting'. The brew was carried round in a bowl of some kind – the earliest of hard or easily cleaned wood.

Then in the 19th century the Ewenny pottery produced their famous twelve-handled pottery casseroles, to be filled with cake and baked apple soaked in beer or cider and hot spices 'from India'. Decorated with birds, berries and oak leaves, those remaining today are highly prized – as many wassail bowls were probably dropped and smashed by the drunken revellers. Interestingly, at the Gwili Pottery near Carmarthen, the art of making wassail bowls has recently been revived.

The geese are getting fat...

In winters past, droves of geese would have been a common sight in areas of west Wales. Between Michaelmas and Christmas, they would be driven down from the Pumpsaint area, fattening themselves on oat gleanings as they neared Carmarthen town. Just south of the town at Llanllwch is 'a field of geese', Maesgwyddau, where the birds were 'shoed' before embarkation at Laugharne. The Tywi estuary south of the castle was known locally as Gosport. It was from there, and from Oxwich Point on the Gower (the path to the shingle beach was known as Gander Street), that the flocks were shipped at high-tide to the Somerset coast and to the wealthy port of Bristol, providing fresh poultry for the festive tables of bankers, ship-owners and city merchants.

The feet of the birds were protected on their comparatively long journeys through the Carmarthenshire lanes by a covering of tar and fine sand, or sometimes crushed oyster shells. Geese were also driven 'on short stilts' – when blunt spikes were inserted into the tarred soles of the unfortunate fowls!

Christmas Eve englyn...

Liw nos, a'n carolau'n hen, fe wenaf
innau'n llawn cenfigen
ar y plant a welant wên
mab y saer ymhob seren.

Ceri Wyn Jones

It's late, the carols are tiring,
but still I'm enviously smiling
at children who see from afar
the carpenter's son in each star.

The *englyn* is one of the most enduring traditional Welsh stanza-forms. A concise and resonant four-line verse, it employs the intricate patterns of rhyme and alliteration known in Welsh as *cynghanedd*.

A Christmas hymn from Pantycelyn

Hallowed be your name always,
My God, my Father, my Christ;
Let your praise be sung by men
As numerous as beads of dew;
Oh, that each blade of grass might be a golden harp
Strung to sing of Mary's child
Born in Bethlehem's stable.

(trans. 'Fy Nuw, fy Nhad, fy Iesu')

William Williams, the son of a farmer, was brought up by his widowed mother in Pantycelyn farmhouse, in Carmarthenshire, in the nineteenth century. Ever since, its name has become synonymous with this famous poet, preacher and hymnwriter. Many of his inspiring hymns, including the instantly recognisable 'Guide me O Thou Great Jehovah', sung to the tune 'Cwm Rhondda', still resound today in churches and chapels, concert halls and sports stadiums across Wales and the world.

A Child's Christmas in Wales...

It was on the afternoon of the Christmas Eve, and I was in Mrs Prothero's garden, waiting for cats, with her son Jim. It was snowing. It was always snowing at Christmas. December, in my memory, is white as Lapland, though there were no reindeers. But there were cats. Patient, cold and callous, our hands wrapped in socks, we waited to snowball the cats. Sleek and long as jaguars and horrible-whiskered, spitting and snarling, they would slink and slide over the white back-garden walls, and the lynx-eyed hunters, Jim and I, fur-capped and mocassined trappers from Hudson Bay, off Mumbles Road, would hurl our deadly snowballs at the green of their eyes. The wise cats never appeared.

Dylan Thomas

Let holly have the mastery...

Come friends raise a song together
A song of praise for the greenwood tree
Lovely wood, and worth its name
And that it is the holly.
Fal di roo di lam tam
Trooli riddle me ree
Trala lamtam talam tani
Lovely wood and worth its name
And that it is the holly.

Traditional folk song

Traditionally holly is master of the greenwood, the dominant tree, and ivy is his female subordinate – or so legend says.

Perhaps that is why, in a custom peculiar to Wales, men and boys chased women and girls through the streets on St Stephen's Day, armed with bunches of prickly holly, and beat their victims till they bled. Such actions, known as 'holming', were not confined to pagan times, or even the Middle Ages. As late as the 1850s 'female domestics and others of a like class' were being terrorised in the streets of Tenby!

No mistletoe ... no luck

Apparently a fine crop of mistletoe meant a fine crop of corn, and vice versa, according to Welsh farmers in olden times. Now in the 21st century there's a danger of a mistletoe shortage once more, as mistletoe-rustling has become rife, particularly in the Monmouthshire, Torfaen and Newport areas. When unscrupulous thieves make off with complete 'bunches' the plant takes years to re-grow. And as old apple orchards are grubbed up, natural habitats are less common.

Decorating the house with mistletoe and kissing under its white berries are both linked to the Celtic Druids of Wales, who ascribed to this parasitic plant magical properties relating to fertility and childbirth. It is known in Wales as 'Druids' Weed'.

Mistletoe also provided protection against sorcery and witchcraft, and could bring good luck to the dairy! According to Sir James Frazer in *The Golden Bough* people in Wales would feed a branch of mistletoe to the first beast that calved after the first hour of the New Year – to ensure a plentiful supply of milk, cream and butter in the coming year.

A Christmas sampler

Religious samplers were popular in the nineteenth century, but usually depicted Old Testament scenes – often copied from prints and engravings in family bibles.

This unusual New Testament sampler, worked by nineteen-year-old Cathrin Davies of Aperporth, and dated July 31st 1862, includes a delightful picture of the Holy Family, surrounded by colourful floral swags, parrots, butterflies and winged cupids. The whole picture is enclosed by a fancy pink and green floral border.

The canvas ground is embroidered with coloured wools in cross-stitch, with Cathrin's name and details, and the biblical inscriptions – in English above the nativity scene, and in Welsh below – stitched in fine italic script.

Behold the Lamb of God
which taketh away the sin of the world

Cofia yn awr dy Growdwr yn
nyddiau dy ieuengctid cyn dyfod y dyddiau blin

Behold the
Lamb of God which
taketh away the sin of the world

Cofia yn awr dy Greawdwr yn
nyddiau dy ieuengctid cyn dyfod y dyddiau blin

Cathrin Davies aged 19.
July 31. 1862.

A Dream at Sea

On Friday November 25th 1904 *The Cardigan and Tivyside Advertiser* announced that the forthcoming Graphic Christmas number would be containing 'a Welsh story' by Allen Raine (Mrs Puddicombe, Traethsaith).

> John Vaughan......returned after a six month's voyage, far more in love with his promised wife than he had been when he sailed.
>
> Leaving his ship (the *Sea Queen*) at the nearest seaport, he hastened home over the frosty roads, with a heart full of joy and Xmas warmth.
>
> Shan, the old servant had prepared a good tea, and little Grif (the Captain's orphaned nephew) silent with happiness, sat close to "Nwncwl Non" until, tired out with his toys, he went early to bed, and John was free to turn his steps towards Bryn Erw, where Hepzibah, awaiting him, had a bright fire and clean-swept hearth.

Anne Adeliza Puddicombe, formerly of Newcastle Emlyn and London, was a celebrated literary figure, in west Wales and beyond. Her innovative romances, such as *A Welsh Singer* (1897) and *Torn Sails* (1898) had become bestsellers and any new stories would have been eagerly awaited.

The Christmas tree

It shone, it sparkled, it was bright
With all the stars of Christmas night,
And every child that came to see
And wonder at that shining tree
Made it more radiant, for those eyes
Lent it the joy of Paradise.

Idris Davies
December 1947

Hunting the little wren (dryw bach)

From Amlwch to Kidwelly and from Llanrhaeadr-ym-Mochant to Marloes there are written records of the strange Christmas tradition of hunting the wren, accompanied by repetitive nonsense jingles, such as the Tenby 'Cutty Wren' song. 'Cutty', a dialect English word means, 'little' and its Welsh form is 'cwta'.

The capture of up to twenty birds (usually on Boxing Day) preceded a strange procession on Twelfth Night, when four burly villagers would 'struggle' with a small, house-shaped bier, bedecked with ribbons, glass windows and a door, enclosing the choicest wren, held high on four poles. At each farm visited they demanded refreshment from the mistress there – or from one of the bearers' sweethearts.

By the time this custom reached Cardiff in the nineteenth century, a bottle of spirits had been added to the holly branch!

> The Wran, the Wran that you may see
> Here guarded on our Holly Tree,
> A bunch of ribbons by his side,
> And a bottle of whiskey to be his guide.

THE CUTTY WREN

O where are you going? says Mil·der to

Mel·der, O where are you

go·ing? says the

younger to the

el·der; O I can·not tell says

Fes·tel to Fose; We're going to the

woods said John the Red Nose, We're

going to the woods said John the Red Nose.

Christmas Revels…

Heaven's bounty on earth in Bachelldref,
  Where there is a song-fest each Christmas,
And a crowd of kinfolk, and a lake of liquor . . .

. . . And the sound of strings and a deluge of drinks,
  And reciting of well-known poems,
And numerous foods, sweet provisions,
  And thick sugar-coated dishes,
And keeping open house for the whole Isle of Honey,
  Clearly none could suppose that there is a court
Like the genial court for honour and grandeur,
  And good-natured well-mannered nobility,
And presiding each day in much prosperity.

A translation by Joseph Clancy from the Welsh of
Dafydd Bach ap Madog Wladaidd, 14th century

Blooms in the snow . . .

Latin name: galanthus nivalis

English names: snowdrop
February fairmaids
Candlemas bells (Feast of Candlemas – Feb 2nd)
Eve's tears
Mary's taper
snow piercer (*cf* French – *perce-niege*)
dingle-dangle

Welsh names: eirlys
lili wen fach (little white lily)
tlws yr eira (snow gem)
cloch maban (baby's bell)
blodyn yr eira (snow flower)

The Nativity Play

It is, at Christmas, a rite that
The children of the vestry
Present in our chapel
The drama of the nativity.

Some adults will have been
Stitching Christmas into old shirts
Old sheets, old curtains
To clothe that gang of thespians.

(from *Drama'r Nadolig* by Gwyn Thomas)

Calennig on New Year's Day...

Calennig (from the word *calan,* the first day of a season or month) was either the small decorated apple presented at a neighbour's door by children, or the actual coins given in return for greeting on the first day of the New Year (before noon, of course!). Here are rhyming instructions on how to make a calennig, the precursor of the well-known Christingle.

Take an apple red and firm, and with a skewer gently turn
To fix three legs of hazel wood, and a fourth for a handle, strong and good.

Next take ears of harvest wheat – stick in the apple, sharp and neat
Reminding us of autumn storm, of harvest home and golden corn.

Add some firs and evergreen, red holly berries that you've seen
To make your Calennig fair and bright, and twinkle in the candlelight.

Now to prove that winter's here, when days are chill and nights are clear,
Sprinkle flour just to show that your Calennig's touched with snow.

And now it's time to knock on wood, greeting neighbours as we should;
It's New Year's Day – if you have any, give us please Calennig penny!

Jolly skating weather ...

Winter weather has always had its compensations – frozen lakes and rivers may have meant trouble and hardship for some in our grandparents' time, but for others they provided a chance for free sport and welcome entertainment. There were no risk assessments needed for a visit to Cilgerran in the 1890s when the river froze over! And skates were most certainly the most sensible footwear for travelling down the canal at Llechryd in a late Victorian winter.

Today, of course, we don't have to wait for wintry weather – ice is available twenty-four-seven in our cities, when millions of litres of water can be frozen to order. The Christmas ice rink has become a popular annual attraction in Cardiff Civic Centre. Visits to the Winter Wonderland and skating parties have been added to the traditional list of seasonal treats, like the pantomime, the pre-Christmas shopping nights, and the chance to meet Santa Claus in his High Street grotto.

A double new year's celebration...

Come to the Gwaun on New Year's night
There's a welcome just for you
As the valley comes to life again
Raise your glasses of 'home brew'!

Only in Wales it seems is the New Year celebrated twice in January – once on January 1st when the double-headed Roman God Janus looks both ways, and once (if you happen to live in the Gwaun Valley, near Fishguard, in Llandysul or on Bardsey Island) on Old New Year's Day, January 13th, *(Hen Galan)* which predates the 1752 change from Julian to Gregorian calendars.

Old New Year's Eve festivities have been vigorously revived in Cwm Gwaun, where local carols are sung to familiar folk tunes, but the riotous free-for-all football match formerly played either on horseback or on foot between the goalposts of Llandysul and Llanwenog churches (8 miles apart) has long since been abandoned. On the Llŷn peninsula, some older folk still refer to Calendr Enlli, the Bardsey calendar.

The Mari Lwyd...

A bleached horse's skull, dug up annually before the Christmas festivities, and reburied after the fun was over, formed the centrepiece of one of the most bizarre customs of south Wales in winter. Thought by some to be linked to medieval hobby-horses and hooded men, and by others to refer to St Mary, the 'mari' or 'mare' might, we are told, even be the same female monster found in the English word 'nightmare'.

A white-sheeted man, holding the brightly ribboned and glass-eyed skull high above him, and operating its jaws by means of a spring, was led by a procession of lads and men from door to door, instigating a musical dispute between themselves and the female occupants, until finally they would be allowed inside for refreshments.

Today Mari Lwyd parties, with a fiddle-playing 'Merryman' and a stick-bearing 'Leader' holding the reins, have revived this Mummer-style festivity and visit hostelries on New Year's Eve – demanding beer and ale, and chasing the girls with the snapping teeth of the Mari Lwyd, the old grey mare.

Wetting the plough ... with Christmas ale

When the plough, symbol of wintertime agricultural life, was 'laid up' over the festivities, often it would be drawn into the farmhouse and placed under the scrubbed table where the family ate. When Christmas beer was passed around, the plough was wetted, a few drops tossed respectfully in its direction.

And the Christmas beer was something special – much stronger than usual, and often brewed on the homestead. Although home-brewing was perfectly legal, the making of malt was not so, but many farmers dodged the malt taxes (and the Excise men) by processing the necessary barley in secret.

"Sometimes the barley was wetted in some secret place in a vessel. At other times it was put in a sack and tied up and thrown into a deep pond of water with a rope fastened thereto in order to land it on terra firma when required . . . sometimes the malt was made in a cottage house underneath the bed, sometimes under a bed of furze . . . and times without number in country churches without any fear of detection."

Heads were finally cleared and work recommenced on Plough Monday, the first Monday after the 6th of January.

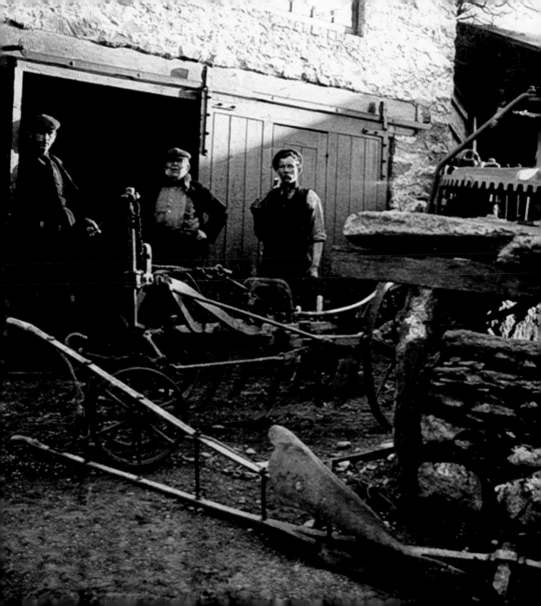

Acknowledgements

The author and publishers gratefully acknowledge permission
to use images and extracts as noted below:

p.2 copper robin, Tim Bowen Antiques; p.5 robin, © Mike Davies; p.7 candles on wood
© www.shawstephens.com; p. 6 'Lost Christmas' published in *Young and Old*, R. S. Thomas,
Chatto and Windus 1972; p.9 three trees painting, © Stella Watras; p.13 geese © Brett
Breckon; p.17, stained glass, 'Ariel' by Angharad Whitfield, www.breconstainedglass.co.uk;
p.18 extract from *A Child's Christmas in Wales*, Dylan Thomas, Dent 1955, reproduced by
permission of David Higham Associates; p.19 snowballs illustration © Ian Benfold Haywood;
p.25 sampler, National Museum and Galleries of Wales; p.27 schooner illustration © Claudia
Myatt; p.28 'The Christmas Tree' published in *Collected Poems of Idris Davies*, ed Islwyn
Jenkins, Gomer 1972; p.29 Christmas tree, Pembrokeshire Museum Service; p.31 calligraphy
© Shirley Norman; p.33 banquet scene, Ruthin Castle; p.35 snowdrop © Llinos Lanini,
www.lliniau.com; p.37 angel illustration © Jac Jones; p. 41 Cardiff Winter Wonderland,
Cardiff City Council; p.42 Bardsey island / Ynys Enlli © Colin Evans; p.45 Mari Lwyd, Ysgol
Cas-blaidd; p.47 Cynwyd smithy, Denbighshire Records Office; cover illustration: Nativity
lovespoon by Paul Curtis.